TALES OF HORROR
MONSTERS

by Jim Pipe

BEARPORT
PUBLISHING

New York, New York

Credits

Linda Bucklin: 4–5; Corbis: 18–19; Christian Darkin 28; Domhnall Dods: 20–21; Everrett/Rex Features: Cover, Title Page, 26–27; Rudolf Georg: 26; Getty: 6, 7; Chris Harvey: 8; Anastasiya Igolkina: 16; Manoj Jethani: 28–29; Milos Jokic: 25 (chicken); Adrian T Jones: 17; LEACH: 4; Ritu Shutterstock: 9, 12, 14, 14–15, 25 (lizard); Johan Swanepoel: 30; ticktock Media image archive: 10, 10–11, 12–13, 19, 20, 22, 24; Alex Tomlinson: 8; Marina Cano Trueba: 31; © Universal/Everrett/Rex Features: 22–23.

Every effort has been made to trace the copyright holders and we apologize in advance for any unintentional omissions. We would be pleased to insert the appropriate acknowledgment in any subsequent edition of this publication.

Library of Congress Cataloging-in-Publication Data

Pipe, Jim.
  Monsters / by Jim Pipe.
    p. cm. — (Tales of horror)
  Includes index.
  ISBN-13: 978-1-59716-204-3 (library binding)
  ISBN-10: 1-59716-204-3 (library binding)
  ISBN-13: 978-1-59716-211-1 (pbk.)
  ISBN-10: 1-59716-211-6 (pbk.)
  1. Monsters. I. Title. II. Series: Pipe, Jim. Tales of horror.

  GR825.P56 2007
  001.944 — dc22

                          2006014420

For more information, write to Bearport Publishing Company, Inc., 101 Fifth Avenue, Suite 6R, New York, New York 10003. Printed in the United States of America.

10 9 8 7 6 5 4 3 2 1

The Tales of Horror series was originally developed by ticktock Media Ltd.

Table of Contents

What Is a Monster?

As the ground begins to shake, a loud roar comes from the distance. Suddenly, a giant creature crashes through the trees. A monster is on the loose!

Most monsters, and there are many kinds, have certain things in common. Many of them are very big—sometimes big enough to eat a human in one bite. Almost all monsters are scary looking. Many of them are also dangerous because of their huge claws or razor-sharp teeth. Some monsters even breathe fire!

For centuries, people have told stories about one-eyed giants, fire-breathing dragons, and birds with human heads. Are the stories true? Are any of the monsters real? Read on and decide for yourself.

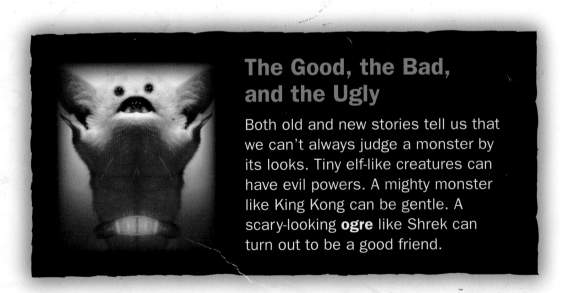

The Good, the Bad, and the Ugly

Both old and new stories tell us that we can't always judge a monster by its looks. Tiny elf-like creatures can have evil powers. A mighty monster like King Kong can be gentle. A scary-looking **ogre** like Shrek can turn out to be a good friend.

5

Scary or Shy?

Monsters may be nasty and scary, but they can also be shy. In general, they avoid towns and cities. Wild, lonely places such as forests, swamps, and deserts are their usual **habitats**.

One famous monster has been spotted on **remote** mountains across the world. In Asia, this shy creature is known as the Yeti (YEH-tee). In North America, it is called Bigfoot or Sasquatch (SASS-kwoch).

In September 1967, rancher Roger Patterson filmed a tall, shaggy creature in the mountains of Northern California. It looked straight at the camera, then vanished. Was this Bigfoot? No one knows, since no other photos of this kind of creature exist.

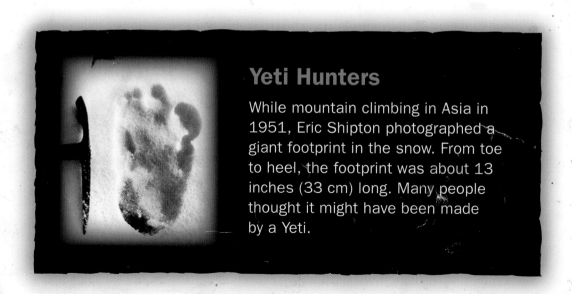

Yeti Hunters

While mountain climbing in Asia in 1951, Eric Shipton photographed a giant footprint in the snow. From toe to heel, the footprint was about 13 inches (33 cm) long. Many people thought it might have been made by a Yeti.

Monster Hunts

Every year, **expeditions** go in search of monsters like the Yeti. **Trackers** look for unusual marks on the ground. Scientists use hi-tech equipment to search for the creatures at night.

For hundreds of years, people have believed that a monster named "Nessie" lives in Loch Ness (LOK NESS), a lake in Scotland. During searches over the past 70 years, many photographs have been snapped showing strange shapes in the lake's water.

Some believe Nessie is actually a giant sea **reptile**, like those that lived during the time of the dinosaurs. In 1987, Operation Deepscan detected a large shape under the water using **sonar equipment**. Could this be Nessie, still in hiding after so many years?

The Death Worm

In 2005, an expedition went deep into the Gobi Desert to search for the "Mongolian Death Worm." Local people reported seeing a fat red worm about three feet (1 m) long. They said it spat out a deadly yellow poison!

9

Beware of Giants

Giants are huge and strong. Many are also **ancient**.

Greek **myths** tell about one kind of giant called the Cyclops (SYE-klops). It had one enormous eye in the middle of its forehead. In the **Middle Ages**, some people claimed they had dug up some Cyclops skulls. It turned out that the skulls belonged to elephants. The "eye **socket**" in each of these skulls was actually the hole for the elephant's trunk!

Giants play a big part in fairy tales, too. In stories such as "Jack and the Beanstalk," they are mean and not very smart. They also love the taste of human flesh. Fortunately, the fairy-tale giants stay home a lot of the time—counting their treasure.

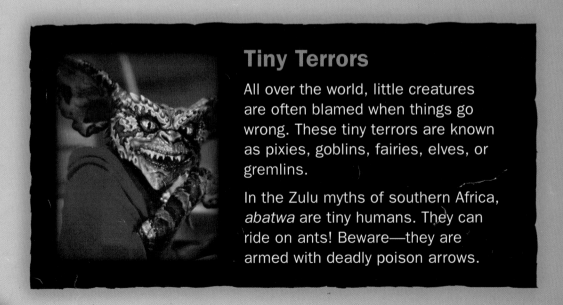

Tiny Terrors

All over the world, little creatures are often blamed when things go wrong. These tiny terrors are known as pixies, goblins, fairies, elves, or gremlins.

In the Zulu myths of southern Africa, *abatwa* are tiny humans. They can ride on ants! Beware—they are armed with deadly poison arrows.

Mixed-Up Monsters

Many monsters are made from the parts of different creatures. In 2001, news stories from New Delhi, India, reported that a vicious beast had been spotted. It was half man and half monkey. The creature stood about four feet (1.2 m) tall and had glowing red eyes.

Some of the scariest monsters are part-human, part-beast. The Sphinx (SFINKS), which appears in Greek myths, had the head of a woman and the body of a lion. It wouldn't let people pass by until they had answered a question. It strangled anyone who got the answer wrong.

Centaurs (SEN-torz) also appeared in ancient myths. These fierce creatures had the head and chest of a human and the body of a horse. Their food was raw flesh.

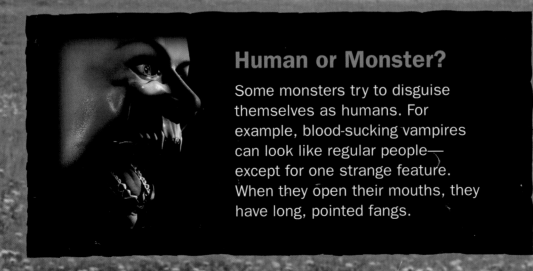

Human or Monster?

Some monsters try to disguise themselves as humans. For example, blood-sucking vampires can look like regular people—except for one strange feature. When they open their mouths, they have long, pointed fangs.

Fierce and Fiery

For hundreds of years, people in Europe lived in fear of dragons. These evil, fire-breathing monsters had the claws of a lion, a spiky tail, scaly skin, and wings like a bat. Did these monsters ever really exist?

The first dragon stories were most likely larger-than-life tales about real-life reptiles. The Roman historian Pliny described giant lizards living in India that attacked and killed elephants. These creatures were probably crocodiles. The famous Italian explorer Marco Polo wrote about dragon bones he had seen in China. These giant bones were probably dinosaur **fossils**.

Living Dragons?

In 1910, European explorers found a giant lizard on an Indonesian island. It was a scaly, scary-looking animal. So they named it the Komodo (kuh-MOH-doh) dragon.

The Komodo can grow up to ten feet (3 m) long. Komodo dragons have poisonous **saliva** and have killed more than 25 people in the last 70 years.

Monsters of the Sky

Dragons aren't the only flying terrors. Other deadly-looking monsters have also swooped down from the sky.

A Harpy is a winged monster from Greek mythology. It is half woman and half bird with sharp claws.

Mothman is a modern monster. The creature was first spotted in November 1966 in West Virginia by five men digging a grave. Suddenly, something flew over them. It was brown, had red eyes, and looked human. Over the next few weeks, there were other **sightings** of this creature. Some people think it was a great horned owl. Could anyone mistake an owl for a human being, though?

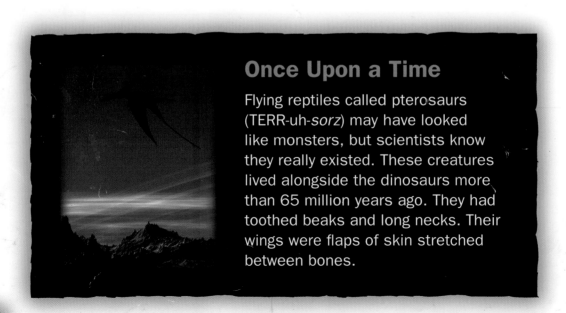

Once Upon a Time

Flying reptiles called pterosaurs (TERR-uh-*sorz*) may have looked like monsters, but scientists know they really existed. These creatures lived alongside the dinosaurs more than 65 million years ago. They had toothed beaks and long necks. Their wings were flaps of skin stretched between bones.

Monsters of the Deep

In the 1700s, Dutch captain Jean Magnus Dens reported a strange incident. He was sailing off the coast of West Africa. Suddenly, two huge arms rose up out of the waves and snatched two of his sailors. Hardly anyone believed his story. Then, in the 1940s, a giant squid was discovered. This sea creature can grow up to around 60 feet (18 m). Could this squid have been the monster that grabbed the sailors?

Few places are as mysterious as the deep ocean. In places it is 6 miles (9.6 km) deep. However, scientists are beginning to explore these cold, dark waters.

What have they found? In March 2006, an eyeless crab-like animal covered in silky blond fur was discovered in the South Pacific. It was more than 1.2 miles (2 km) below the surface.

Swimming with Sharks

Many people think of great white sharks as real-life monsters. The largest of these fierce fish have up to 3,000 teeth and are more than 15 feet (4.5 m) long. Although they do sometimes go after people, shark attacks are rare. In fact, falling coconuts kill 15 times more people each year than sharks do!

From Human to Monster

How do certain people become monsters? In some stories, they are born that way. In other tales, they have special powers that allow them to change their appearance.

In the Middle Ages, witches were widely feared. It was believed they had the power to turn themselves into werewolves and vampires. Anyone suspected of being a witch was put on trial. Thousands of innocent people were put to death.

Today, many comic book characters are humans with the power to turn themselves into monsters. One of Spiderman's enemies, the Lizard, is scientist Curt Connors. After taking a powerful drug, Connors grows into a two-legged reptile. He has tough scales, sharp teeth and claws, and a powerful tail.

A Bad Hair Day

In Greek myths, the gods often punish people by changing their appearance. Medusa (mih-DOO-suh) was a young woman with beautiful hair. The goddess Athena (uh-THEE-nuh) became jealous of Medusa. So she changed Medusa's hair into snakes. Anyone who looked at her after that turned into stone.

Science Monsters

Sometimes monsters are made when science experiments go wrong. In Mary Shelley's book *Frankenstein*, a scientist sews together parts from dead bodies to make a monster. Then he uses electricity to shock the creature to life.

In The Incredible Hulk comic books and movies, scientist Bruce Banner is poisoned by **radiation**. As a result, he turns into a green giant whenever he gets angry.

Another scientist gets into trouble in the movie *The Fly*. After he mixes his **genes** with those from a fly, he becomes half man, half fly. Like a real fly, he has to spit on his food to **liquefy** it before he can eat it!

Robot Monsters

Thanks to modern technology, robots are becoming more like humans. One kind of robot is even being used to perform **surgery**. Some people are afraid that robots could take over the world, however. In the movie *The Terminator*, a killer robot that feels no fear or pain comes back from the future. It is unstoppable!

Monster Tales

Over the years, writers have dreamed up all sorts of monsters. They have written about evil vampires, scary-looking **mutants**, killer robots, and eerie **aliens**.

Some of the oddest monsters in books date back to the Middle Ages. Back then, monks decorated their books with beasts such as the basilisk (BAZ-uh-lisk). This evil creature looked like a cross between a chicken and a snake!

Many of the most famous monster stories were written during the 1800s. Today, most people have heard of the books *Frankenstein* (1818), *The Hunchback of Notre Dame* (1831), and *Dracula* (1897). Movies about their creepy main characters are still being made.

Monsters of Modern Times

Robots and aliens invaded **science fiction** during the 1900s. In John Wyndham's book *The Day of the Triffids* (1951), giant flesh-eating plants that traveled on meteors from space try to take over the world.

Robots turn against humans in Karel Capek's play *Rossum's Universal Robots* (1920). The word "robot" was first introduced in this play.

25

Movie Monsters

Monsters have kept moviegoers screaming for a long time. In many early movies, such as *Frankenstein* (1931), *The Wolf Man* (1941), and *The Mummy's Tomb* (1942), the monstrous main characters were played by actors in costumes. In some other early movies, such as *King Kong* (1933), filmmakers used models to create giant monsters on screen.

In the 1950s, models were also used to make movies about Godzilla (god-ZIL-uh). In the film *Godzilla: King of the Monsters* (1956), this monster lizard is awakened by an **atomic bomb** exploding in the Pacific Ocean.

Today, computers can create amazing monsters on screen. In the recent remake of *King Kong* (2005), a 25-foot (8-m) **computer-generated** gorilla fights fierce, equally large computer-generated dinosaurs.

They Came from Outer Space!

Many movies feature monsters from space. In the 1950s and 1960s, "B movies" were full-length films that were made for very little money. The moviemakers tried to make scary aliens using turkeys, lobsters, and dogs.

Natural-Born Killers

With its huge teeth and razor-sharp claws, *T. rex* once roamed over parts of North America. Luckily for people, the mighty meat-eater died out about 65 million years ago, along with lots of other scary dinosaurs.

A few ancient hunters have survived, however. Large crocodiles can kill sharks, lions, and buffaloes. Humans are also on the menu! The crocs wait silently in the water before grabbing their victims and drowning them.

Attacks on people by big **predators** are rare. Still, there are some scary animals out there. Sometimes sharks bite surfers, bears maul campers, and tigers attack remote villages.

A Dinosaur Survivor?

In the swampy forests of western Africa, many people have reported seeing a strange elephant-sized creature. It has smooth, brownish skin, a long neck and tail, and three-clawed feet the size of frying pans.

Some monster-hunters believe that this creature, called Mokele-Mbembe by local people, may be a living dinosaur. Since 1980, more than 20 expeditions have gone in search of this shy creature, but the beast hasn't turned up—yet!

Do Monsters Exist?

Some monsters may exist only in myths. However, myths are based on real events and real fears. In the past, people used these traditional stories to explain the world around them. They thought that an earthquake was caused by a giant moving around underground. Or, a **whirlpool** was created by a sea monster trying to suck sailors into the deep ocean. Or, lightning was the result of dragons fighting in the sky.

Modern monsters such as the Yeti might be real rather than mythical. They are probably not as frightful as we think, however. The Yeti might just be a large bear or a rare gorilla. Over time, however, it has grown in our imagination into a real-life monster!

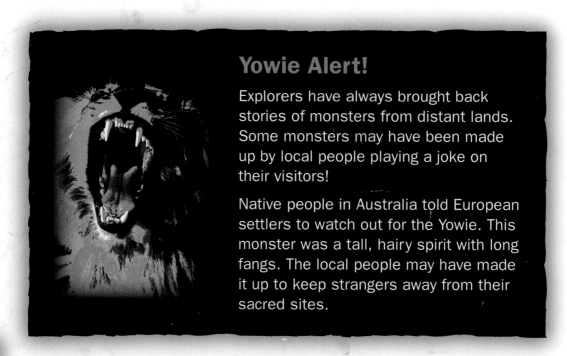

Yowie Alert!

Explorers have always brought back stories of monsters from distant lands. Some monsters may have been made up by local people playing a joke on their visitors!

Native people in Australia told European settlers to watch out for the Yowie. This monster was a tall, hairy spirit with long fangs. The local people may have made it up to keep strangers away from their sacred sites.

31

Glossary

aliens (AY-lee-uhnz) beings from faraway places, such as outer space

ancient (AYN-shunt) very old

atomic bomb (uh-TOM-ik BOM) an extremely powerful and destructive type of bomb

computer-generated (kuhm-PYOO-tur JEN-uh-*rate*-id) made by computer technology

expeditions (*ek*-spuh-DISH-uhnz) long trips taken for a specific reason, such as exploring

fossils (FOSS-uhlz) what is left of plants or animals that lived long ago

genes (JEENZ) tiny parts of a person or animal that determine characteristics such as body size and eye color

habitats (HAB-uh-*tats*) places where creatures live

liquefy (LIK-wuh-fye) to turn into liquid

Middle Ages (MID-uhl AYJ-iz) the period of European history from about AD 500 to 1500

mutants (MYOOT-uhnts) living beings that are very different from others of their kind

myths (MITHS) traditional stories that often tell of larger-than-life beings and mysterious events

ogre (OH-gur) an ugly giant

predators (PRED-uh-turz) animals that hunt other animals for food

radiation (*ray*-dee-AY-shuhn) a form of energy that can be very dangerous when not properly controlled

remote (ri-MOHT) far from any settled place

reptile (REP-tile) a cold-blooded animal that usually has dry, scaly skin, such as a lizard, snake, turtle, or crocodile

saliva (suh-LYE-vuh) the liquid in the mouths of humans and animals that helps them swallow and chew

science fiction (SYE-uhnss FIK-shuhn) made-up stories that explore the effect that science has on people and their world

sightings (SITE-ings) occasions when people have seen something

socket (SOK-it) a hole found in a skull

sonar equipment (SOH-nar i-KWIP-muhnt) gear used to locate objects underwater

surgery (SUR-jer-ee) the part of medical science that focuses on cutting open the body to fix something inside

trackers (TRAK-urz) people who search for a particular thing

whirlpool (WURL-pool) water that moves in a circle and can pull objects in

Index